WELCOME TO MY COUNTRY

Welcome to
SOUTH KOREA

Gareth Stevens Publishing
A WORLD ALMANAC EDUCATION GROUP COMPANY

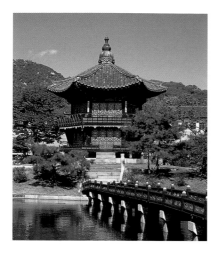

Written by
KAREN KWEK/JOHANNA MASSE

Edited by
MELVIN NEO

Edited in USA by
DOROTHY L. GIBBS

Designed by
GEOSLYN LIM

Picture research by
SUSAN JANE MANUEL

First published in North America in 2003 by
Gareth Stevens Publishing
A World Almanac Education Group Company
330 West Olive Street, Suite 100
Milwaukee, Wisconsin 53212 USA

Please visit our web site at:
www.garethstevens.com
For a free color catalog describing
Gareth Stevens Publishing's list of high-quality
books and multimedia programs,
call 1-800-542-2595 (USA) or
1-800-387-3178 (Canada).
Gareth Stevens Publishing's fax: (414) 332-3567.

© TIMES MEDIA PRIVATE LIMITED 2003
Originated and designed by
Times Editions
An imprint of Times Media Private Limited
A member of the Times Publishing Group
Times Centre, 1 New Industrial Road
Singapore 536196
http://www.timesone.com.sg/te

Library of Congress Cataloging-in-Publication Data
Kwek, Karen.
Welcome to South Korea / Karen Kwek and Johanna Masse.
p. cm. — (Welcome to my country)
Summary: An overview of the geography, history,
government, economy, people, and culture of South Korea.
Includes bibliographical references and index.
ISBN 0-8368-2553-5 (lib. bdg.)
1. Korea (South)—Juvenile literature. [1. Korea (South).]
I. Masse, Johanna, 1976– . II. Title. III. Series.
DS902.K879   2003
951.95—dc21   2002044534

Printed in Singapore

1 2 3 4 5 6 7 8 9 07 06 05 04 03

PICTURE CREDITS
A.N.A. Press Agency: 13
Art Directors & TRIP Photo Library: 1, 4,
   21, 23, 25, 28
Camera Press: 5, 17
Downtown Money Point: 44
Alain Evrard: 3 (center), 9 (bottom), 18,
   19, 20, 41 (both)
Focus Team – Italy: 7, 38, 40
Getty Images/HultonArchive: 14,
   15 (bottom), 37
Haga Library, Japan: cover, 3 (bottom),
   22, 35 (both), 43, 45
HBL Network Photo Agency: 24
Korea National Tourism Organization:
   3 (top), 8, 9 (top), 10, 11, 15 (top),
   16, 26, 27 (top), 29, 30, 33, 34, 36, 39
North Wind Picture Archives: 12, 27 (bottom)
Kay Shaw Photography: 2, 6, 31
Topham Picturepoint: 32

Digital Scanning by Superskill Graphics Pte Ltd

Contents

Words that appear in the glossary are printed in **boldface** type the first time they occur in the text.

Welcome to South Korea!

The Korean **peninsula** has long been overshadowed by China and Japan, its powerful neighbors, yet Koreans have held on fiercely to a culture all their own. The peninsula was divided into North Korea and South Korea in 1948. Let's learn more about South Korea.

Opposite: These buildings are part of the fortress that once protected the city of Hanyang, which is now called Seoul.

Below: Korean children enjoy their country's many colorful festivals.

The Flag of South Korea

The South Korean flag has a white background with four groups of black lines, called **trigrams**, around a perfectly divided red and blue circle. The trigrams represent harmony. The circle symbolizes balance in the universe.

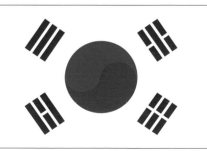

The Land

South Korea occupies 37,900 square miles (98,161 square kilometers) at the bottom of the Korean peninsula. The country also includes thousands of tiny islands. These islands are actually the tops of underwater mountains. Except to the north, South Korea is surrounded by water. The Sea of Japan is to the east, and the Yellow Sea is to the west. North Korea, China, and Japan are South Korea's closest neighbors.

Below: South Korea's rivers are very important for both electricity and **irrigation.** The Han River, which flows through the capital city of Seoul, is also important for transportation.

Mountains and highlands cover more than two-thirds of South Korea. The country has two main mountain ranges. The Taebaek range is along the northeastern coast. The Sobaek range runs, north to south, through the middle of the country. South Korea's highest point, Mount Halla, is on Cheju Island, which is the country's largest island. The longest river, the Naktong, flows north to south for 325 miles (523 km).

Above: Soraksan National Park's beautiful scenery attracts many visitors, especially mountain climbers, to the Kangwon province during every season of the year.

Climate

South Korea has a **humid** climate and four separate seasons. Spring, which lasts from April to June, has warm, sunny weather. Summer, from June to September, is hot and rainy. Late summer sometimes brings typhoons, which are strong storms with heavy rain and high winds. Autumn, from September through December, is followed by a mild, dry winter from January to March.

Below: During autumn in South Korea, the leaves change from green to red and gold. These beautiful autumn leaves are in the Secret Garden of the Changdok Palace in the city of Seoul.

Left: South Korea's national flower, the Rose of Sharon, brightens up the countryside all through summer.

Plants and Animals

Many kinds of trees, including birch, oak, spruce, and pine, grow in South Korea. Fruit trees such as apple, pear, and Chinese **quince** are very common. The world's oldest fruit tree, a **gingko** over a thousand years old, can be found in South Korea's Kyonggi province.

Weasels are one of many kinds of small animals living in South Korea's forests. Today, large animals, such as bears and leopards, have become rare.

Below: The Korean tiger once roamed the peninsula in great numbers, but this large animal now appears more often in traditional Korean paintings.

9

History

About two thousand years ago, the Chinese controlled much of the Korean peninsula. In the first century B.C., however, Koreans began to form their own kingdoms. From the late third century A.D., three kingdoms, the Koguryo, the Silla, and the Paekche, ruled the peninsula. In 668, the Silla kingdom conquered the other two and ruled all of Korea for 250 years.

Left: Koreans celebrate their past with a parade during the Silla Cultural Festival.

Left:
The Chomsongdae **Observatory**, in North Kyongsang province, was built during the reign (632–647) of the Silla's Queen Sondok. It is the world's oldest observatory.

The Koryo Kingdom

When the power of the Silla kingdom weakened, a **warlord** named Wang Kon defeated the Silla's king and set up the Koryo kingdom. Some people think that *Korea* comes from "Koryo."

In 1392, a rebellious Koryo general overthrew the king and started the Yi **dynasty**. This dynasty changed the name of the country to *Choson*, which means "Land of Morning Calm," and ruled for more than five hundred years.

Foreign Control

In 1894, a group of Koreans rose up against the Choson government. China and Japan sent soldiers to help the government but ended up fighting each other for control of Korea. Japan won and ruled Korea from 1910 until the end of World War II, in 1945. After Japan was defeated in World War II, the Korean peninsula was divided into two separate countries. The Soviet Union controlled North Korea. The United States controlled South Korea.

Above: This picture shows Japanese soldiers landing in Korea in 1904.

War and Military Rule

On June 25, 1950, soldiers from North Korea **invaded** South Korea, starting the Korean War, which lasted until 1953. Nearly three million people died in the war, and many Korean families were forced to leave their homes.

From 1961 to 1981, strict **military** leaders controlled the government of South Korea.

Left: University students in South Korea often hold public **protests** when they do not agree with the government. Police officers must sometimes take strong action to keep protests under control.

A United Korea

During the 1990s, leaders from North Korea and South Korea started talking about **reunification**. On June 13, 2000, South Korean president Kim Dae Jung met with North Korean president Kim Jong-il in P'yongyang, the capital of North Korea. It was the first meeting of this kind between the two countries in fifty years. Many Koreans hope that their countries will soon be one again.

Left: Government officials from North Korea (*left*) and South Korea (*right*) met face to face to talk about reuniting the two countries.

Queen Sondok (?–647)

As ruler of the Silla kingdom from 632 to 647, Queen Sondok encouraged learning and supported education for women. She also established a good relationship with China.

Yi Sun-shin (1545–1598)

Yi Sun-shin

One of Korea's most honored heroes, Admiral Yi Sun-shin invented the first iron-covered warships. He used these ships to defeat a Japanese attack during the Yi dynasty, but he was killed in the battle.

Park Chung Hee (1917–1979)

Park Chung Hee

General Park Chung Hee became the president of South Korea in 1961. Although he developed the country's industries and improved the economy, his strict laws made him unpopular. General Park was **assassinated** on October 26, 1979.

Government and the Economy

South Korea is a democracy, which means that its citizens vote for their own leaders. South Koreans elect a new president every five years. The president is in charge of the country's foreign relations and commands the armed forces. A prime minister, with the help of deputy prime ministers and state council members, runs the day-to-day government.

Left: South Korea's legislature meets at the National Assembly building in Seoul.

South Korea's legislature, called the National Assembly, has 273 members. Most of the members are elected by the people. Each member serves a four-year term. The Assembly makes laws and supervises government agencies.

The judicial branch of South Korea's government includes a Supreme Court and two levels of lower courts. Supreme Court justices serve six-year terms.

From Agriculture to Industry

During their thirty-five years of rule over the Korean peninsula, the Japanese developed agriculture in the south and industry in the north. When the country was divided, South Korea's economy struggled with very limited industrial resources. Today, South Korea has a booming industrial economy, and only about 12 percent of South Koreans work in agriculture.

Below: Not much of the land in South Korea is good for farming, so most farms are small but well run. More than half of the farmland is used to grow rice, but vegetables and barley are important crops, too.

Manufacturing

South Korean factories produce a wide variety of goods, including electronic equipment, cars, clothing, chemicals, and food products. The country is also a world leader in the high-tech industry, which produces computer chips and video games. Since South Korea has few natural resources, its industries often trade manufactured goods for raw materials. Its main trading partners are the United States, Japan, and China.

People and Lifestyle

The first people to live on the Korean peninsula were probably Mongols who traveled there from northeastern China during prehistoric times. Today, about 48 million people live in South Korea. This large number includes very few foreigners. The biggest group of non-Korean people is the Chinese, and they number only about twenty thousand.

Left: Most South Koreans speak the same language and come from the same cultural background so they share many of the same customs and traditions.

Left: Most Korean homes do not have a lot of furniture. People eat at low tables, sitting on their heated floors instead of on chairs. Also, in most Korean homes, people do not wear shoes.

Because South Korea has so many mountains, most of its people live in the southern and western coastal areas or along the country's rivers. More than 75 percent of South Korea's population live in cities. Most South Koreans do not have cars, but convenient public transportation makes traveling easy.

Traditional Korean homes are small, one-story buildings with tiled roofs and clay or stone floors. Hot water pipes under the floors keep the rooms warm when the weather is cold.

Traditional Family Life

In the past, Korean families were very large, and many generations of relatives, including parents, children, aunts, uncles, cousins, grandparents, and even great-grandparents, lived in the same house. The heads of families were always men, usually the father or grandfather, and all other family members obeyed their wishes.

Below: Traditionally, a Korean married a person chosen by his or her parents. Today, Koreans marry for love. This bride and groom's wedding ceremony follows traditional Korean customs.

Left:
In traditional Korean families, having many children was considered a special blessing. Today, the country has limited space for its large population so most families have only one or two children.

Family Life Today

Modern Korean families are very different from those of the past. Most are small, usually just parents and their children. Grandparents and other older relatives are still highly respected but no longer hold traditional family roles. Men and women are treated much more equally, and both husbands and wives commonly work outside the home.

Education

Just over a hundred years ago, only boys from wealthy Korean families went to school. Today, all Korean children have equal opportunities for education.

To learn basic reading and writing skills, children are required to attend six years of elementary school and three years of middle school. At these levels, education is free of charge.

Above: In the late 1800s, missionaries from Western countries brought new ideas about education to South Korea. Yonsei University, in Seoul, was founded in 1885.

High school in South Korea lasts three years and offers students many different kinds of course work. In the second year, a student can choose to focus his or her studies in either arts or sciences or in subjects that provide job training in fields such as business, technology, and agriculture.

More than half of all high school graduates in South Korea continue their education at a college or university. To enter, they must pass both a qualifying state examination and an entrance exam for the college they wish to attend.

Left: For many South Korean children, an elementary school art class is just the start of up to sixteen years of education.

Religion

South Korea's two main religions are Christianity and Buddhism. Although slightly more South Koreans today are Christians, Buddhism is a much older religion. Introduced around 370 A.D., it was the official religion of the Silla dynasty. Buddhists believe that simple living, prayer, and helping others will make them wise, happy, and peaceful.

Below: Buddhists follow the teachings of the Buddha, who was born a prince but left his riches to lead a simple life. Buddhist monks often celebrate the Buddha's birthday with a procession.

The Chinese brought Christianity to South Korea in the 1800s. At first, Korean rulers considered Christianity a foreign religion, and they **persecuted** Christians. By 1882, however, rulers were protecting Christian missionaries, medical workers, and educators.

Many ancient Korean laws and customs are based on Confucianism, which was the most important religion during the Yi dynasty.

CONFUCIUS.

Language

Korean people had no written language, at first. They used characters from the Chinese language to write down their thoughts. In the 1400s, the Korean king had language experts create an alphabet for an official written language, which was called *hangul* (hahn-gool). The hangul alphabet has twenty-four letters. Today, most Koreans speak a form of the hangul language that was used in Seoul around the 1930s.

Left: Many signs in South Korea are written in both hangul and English.

Left: The writing on this monument is a poem by Sambong Jeong Do-jeon, who lived during the Yi dynasty.

Literature

During the Koryo period, short poems with hidden meanings and folktales about everyday life were the most popular forms of literature. Twentieth-century wars and the division of the Korean peninsula have affected the work of modern Korean poets and writers. Kim Chi-ha's poetry shows his disappointment with the country's government. Novelist Park Kyong-ni wrote about the hardships of Koreans under Japanese rule.

Arts

Dancing is one of South Korea's most popular art forms. **Ritual**, folk, and court dances are the three main kinds of traditional dancing. Many ritual dances are Confucian or Buddhist customs passed down by generations of Korean ancestors. Some of these dances are forms of ancestor worship.

Below:
South Koreans often perform ritual dances at temples or during religious festivals.

Korean folk dancing is colorful, lively, and fun to watch. The farmer's dance is one of South Korea's favorite folk dances. Dancers wear brightly colored costumes and hats that have a long white streamer attached at the top. As the dancers jump and spin, they whip their necks around to make the streamers float through the air.

Court dances are slower and more complicated than folk dances. In the past, court dancers performed for noble families on special occasions.

Above:
The farmer's dance, which is performed mostly at agricultural festivals, reminds South Koreans how important farming has been in their country's history.

Music

Korean villagers used to make musical instruments out of wood, stones, string, and other materials around them. Music was probably an important part of their celebrations and rituals. The traditional instruments of South Korea include the *changgo* (chahng-go), which is a drum that is shaped like an hourglass, and the *kayagum* (kie-yah-goom) which is a stringed instrument.

Pottery and Painting

Celadon pottery is an art that began in China, but twelfth-century Korean potters added their own special styles and techniques. This type of pottery has a distinctive bluish green **glaze**.

Between the fifth and the fifteenth centuries, Korean artists produced thousands of images of the Buddha. Then landscape painting and Chinese-style **calligraphy** became popular.

Below: The artwork in most Buddhist temples includes richly detailed paintings of the Buddha and other religious figures.

Leisure

Board Games

South Koreans enjoy playing games. Many of their traditional board games started in China. *Changgi* (chahng-gee) is the Korean form of Chinese chess. Two players each have sixteen game pieces that represent horses, elephants, chariots, soldiers, cannons, and a general. A player wins by capturing the other player's general.

Below: *Paduk* (pah-duke) is a traditional Korean board game played with small black and white stones. Players try to control the board with their stones and capture the other player's stones.

Left: A seesaw in South Korea is usually just a plank of wood resting on a bag of rice straw or a rolled-up mat.

Other Games and Activities

Men in South Korea like to play a rough game called *chajonnori* (chah-john-nor-ee). Players form two teams. Each team carries its leader around on a wooden platform. The first team to knock the other team's leader or their platform to the ground wins the game.

For South Korean women and girls, playing on seesaws has been a favorite activity since ancient times. Flying kites also has a long history in Korea. The oldest kite flying record in the country dates back to 647.

Below: Among the more than seventy kite designs found in South Korea, the shield kite is the most popular. It is made of bamboo sticks covered with mulberry paper. A round hole in the center helps the kite move quickly.

Sports

Soccer and baseball are South Korea's favorite sports. South Korea was the first Asian country with a professional soccer team. The South Korean team has won several medals at the Asian Games, and the country co-hosted a World Cup event with Japan in 2002.

South Korea started a professional baseball league in 1982. In 1984 and 1985, young Korean players won the Little League World Series. In 2000,

Above: Especially on weekends, South Koreans like to go mountain climbing or hiking on mountain trails. Because many mountains are low, the trails are suitable for the whole family.

South Korea beat the United States to win the AAA World Junior Baseball Championship held in Canada.

South Korean women **excel** in archery and won gold medals in both the 1988 and the 1992 Olympics.

Martial Arts

Taekwondo began in Korea over two thousand years ago. This martial art develops strength and speed for self-defense without the use of weapons.

Below: South Korea has had a number of champions in long-distance running. The most recent is Lee Bong-ju (*second from left*), who won the Boston Marathon in 2001.

Happy New Year!

The biggest celebration of the year in South Korea is the New Year festival called *Solnal* (sohl-nahl). It starts on January 1 and lasts three days. During this festival, families play games and eat special foods. South Koreans also celebrate the new **lunar** year, usually in late January or early February. The actual date is determined by the lunar calendar, which is based on the Moon's movement around Earth.

Above: On New Year's Day, South Korean children bow to their parents and older relatives to show their respect. In return, they are given money, cakes, or fruit and advice for the new year.

Other Holidays

South Korea has many holidays that celebrate important historical events. Two of them, Independence Movement Day on March 1 and Liberation Day on August 15, honor events that led to freedom from Japan. South Korean children are honored with awards, gifts, and special activities on May 5, when the country celebrates Children's Day.

Left: In April or May, Buddhists in South Korea celebrate the Buddha's birthday. This event includes decorating shrines with paper lanterns and visiting temples to pray and to hold processions.

Food

Because rice is South Korea's most important crop, it is part of almost every meal. Most Korean meals also include soup and **kimchi** (kim-chee). Some Korean soups are simple broths. Others contain many different kinds of meat, vegetables, and seafood. Kimchi is a cabbage dish that is seasoned with red pepper to make it very spicy.

Below: Koreans eat three meals a day. Each meal includes several side dishes called *panchen* (pahn-chen). The number of panchen increases with each meal of the day.

Left: South Korea is a peninsula so fish and seafood are part of everyone's diet. South Koreans often eat seafood stews and broiled fish.

After meals, Koreans sometimes drink tea to help digest their food. They might also have a dessert of fresh fruit. Sweets are usually eaten only as snacks.

Grilled Favorites

Bulgogi (bull-go-gee) is a popular dish both in and outside the country. It is made with strips of seasoned beef that are grilled over an open fire. *Galbi* (gahl-bee) is another grilled favorite.

Below: At home or in restaurants, South Koreans love grilled meats.

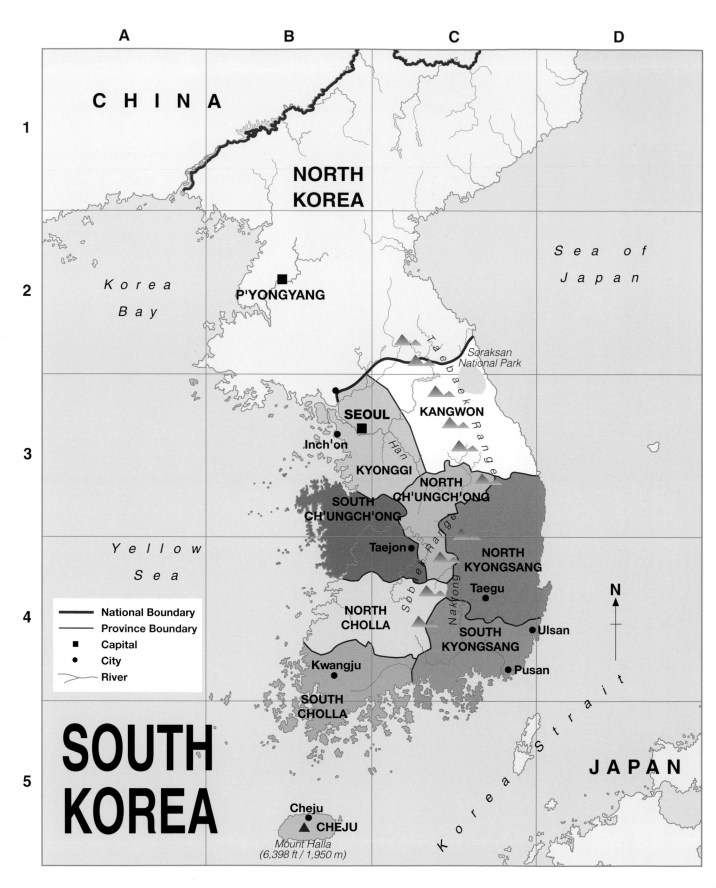

A   **B**   **C**   **D**

1

C H I N A

NORTH
KOREA

2

*Korea
Bay*

■
P'YONGYANG

*S e a   o f
J a p a n*

3

*Soraksan
National Park*

KANGWON

SEOUL ■

● Inch'on

Han

KYONGGI

**NORTH
CH'UNGCH'ONG**

**SOUTH
CH'UNGCH'ONG**

Taebaek Range

4

*Yellow
Sea*

Sobaek Range

Taejon ●

**NORTH
KYONGSANG**

Naktong

Taegu ●

N
↑

**NORTH
CHOLLA**

**SOUTH
KYONGSANG**

Ulsan ●

● Pusan

	National Boundary
	Province Boundary
■	Capital
●	City
～	River

Kwangju ●

5

**SOUTH
KOREA**

**SOUTH
CHOLLA**

Korea Strait

J A P A N

Cheju
● ▲ **CHEJU**
*Mount Halla
(6,398 ft / 1,950 m)*

Above: Korean villages traditionally use carved wooden posts for protection from evil spirits.

Cheju (province/
    city) B5

China A1–C1

Han River B3–C3

Inch'on B3

Japan D5

Kangwon (province)
    C2–C3

Korea Bay A1–A2

Korea Strait
    C5–D4

Kwangju B4

Kyonggi (province)
    B3–C3

Mount Halla B5

Naktong River C4

North Cholla
    (province) B4–C4

North Ch'ungch'ong
    (province) C3–C4

North Korea B3–D1

North Kyongsang
    (province) C3–D4

Pusan C4

P'yongyang B2

Sea of Japan C2–D4

Seoul B3

Sobaek Range
    C3–C4

Soraksan National
    Park C2–C3

South Cholla
    (province) B5–C4

South Ch'ungch'ong
    (province) B3–C4

South Kyongsang
    (province) C4–C5

Taebaek Range
    C2–C3

Taegu C4

Taejon C4

Ulsan C4

Yellow Sea A3–B5

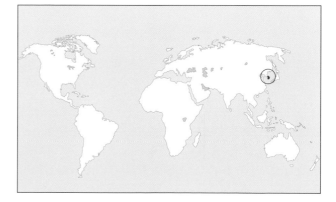

Quick Facts

Official Name   Republic of Korea

Capital   Seoul

Official Language   Korean (hangul)

Population   47,904,370

Land Area   37,900 square miles (98,161 square km)

Provinces   Cheju, Kangwon, Kyonggi, North Cholla, North Ch'ungch'ong, North Kyongsang, South Cholla, South Ch'ungch'ong, South Kyongsang

Major Cities   Inch'on, Kwangju, Pusan, Seoul, Taegu, Taejon, Ulsan

Highest Point   Mount Halla 6,398 feet (1,950 m)

Longest River   Naktong 325 miles (523 km)

Main Religions   Buddhism, Christianity

Major Holidays   New Year's Day (January 1), Lunar New Year (January/February), Independence Movement Day (March 1), Buddha's Birthday (April/May), Children's Day (May 5), Liberation Day (August 15)

Currency   Won (1,186 KRW = U.S. $1 as of 2003)

Opposite: The Changdok Palace is one of five royal palaces in Seoul.

Glossary

assassinated: murdered, usually for political reasons.

bulgogi (bull-go-gee)**:** strips of seasoned beef that are grilled, then mixed with rice and wrapped in a lettuce leaf to be eaten with the hands.

calligraphy: the art of elegant writing or lettering, sometimes using a small brush with fine, pointed bristles.

civilian: a person who is not an active member of a government force, such as the military or the police.

dynasty: a family of rulers who inherit their power.

excel: to be better than others.

galbi (gahl-bee)**:** barbecued beef ribs.

gingko: a decorative shade tree from eastern China that has fan-shaped leaves and yellow fruit.

glaze: a smooth, hard, glossy coating.

humid: damp, usually describing the amount of moisture in the air.

invaded: entered a place in an unfriendly or warlike way to conquer or take over.

irrigation: the process of bringing water from a lake or river through pipes or ditches to an area of land where crops are planted.

kimchi (kim-chee)**:** a kind of pickled salad, made with cabbage and other vegetables and seasoned with red pepper to make it hot and spicy.

lunar: relating to Earth's moon.

military: relating to any armed forces.

observatory: a building with a wide view of the sky and surrounding land for the scientific study of nature.

peninsula: a strip of land surrounded on three sides by water.

persecuted: treated in a cruel and harmful way.

protests: formal actions or statements of disapproval or disagreement by individuals, groups, or organizations.

quince: an Asian tree that belongs to the rose family and has hard, yellow, applelike fruit.

reunification: the process of bringing together again something that has been divided.

ritual: relating to religious ceremonies and practices.

trigrams: groups of three whole or broken lines in any of eight possible combinations.

warlord: a powerful military leader.

More Books to Read

Good-Bye, 382 Shin Dang Dong. Francis Park and Ginger Park (National Geographic)

Kongi and Potgi: A Cinderella Story from Korea. Oki S. Han (Dial Books for Young Readers)

My Freedom Trip. Frances Park and Ginger Park (Boyds Mills Press)

The Rabbit's Tail: A Story from Korea. Suzanne Crowder Han (Henry Holt)

Sing N Learn Korean: Introduce Korean With Favorite Children's Songs. Bo-Kyung Kim and Selina Yoon (Master Communications)

South Korea. Countries of the World series. Lucile Davis (Bridgestone)

South Korea. Festivals of the World series. Ho Siow Yen (Gareth Stevens)

South Korea. Next Stop series. Fred Martin (Heinemann Library)

Videos

Families of Korea. (Master Communications)

Hidden Korea. (PBS Home Video)

Korean-American Heritage. (Schlessinger Media)

South Korea. (Questar)

Web Sites

iml.jou.ufl.edu/projects/STUDENTS/ Hwang/home.htm

www.curriculum.edu.au/accessasia/ korea/kids.htm

www.cwd.go.kr/english/children/ country/index.php

www.shakamak.k12.in.us/cgkids/site/ kid_1093.htm

Due to the dynamic nature of the Internet, some web sites stay current longer than others. To find additional web sites, use a reliable search engine with one or more of the following keywords to help you locate information about South Korea. Keywords: *celadon pottery, Cheju, hangul, Kim Dae Jung, Koryo, Seoul, Silla Kingdom.*

Index